How To Use YouTube To Find Your Videos Targeted Audience!!
What every YouTube Creator Need To Know

Ebonygeek45

Must Read Before You Upload Your Next YouTube Video

Shannon Davis

Author's YouTube Channel at:
Ebonygeek45
And
Tippys Thoughts – Tippys YouTube Tips

TABLE OF CONTENTS

DEDICATION

This book is dedicated to my loyal YouTube Subscribers and YouTube Creators that need help with their YouTube Channel and Videos. The competition is high. But, by knowing how to work with YouTube itself and with the marketing know how, you can get your YouTube Channel and videos discovered. You will see a big improvement you can build on. Keep making good content and you will find success. Above all else, enjoy the Journey.

Ebonygeek45 aka Shannon Davis
Tippy

i

INTRODUCTION

My name is Ebonygeek45, and I have been creating YouTube videos for years.

My focus was not on getting subscribers or even views. My thought process was that if someone saw my videos and like them, they would subscribe. It is not that easy, or everyone would be doing it.

The simple truth is YouTube Subscribers only subscribe if that is their habit. You may get someone to subscribe to your YouTube Channel if they are extremely impressed with your YouTube Videos(But, that is few and far between.).

Starting out, my YouTube Channel was about breaking into something new and exciting. It was about expanding into a new territory and blasting past comfort levels.

As I did more YouTube Videos, I became comfortable instead of nervous every time a new video was started. Amazingly enough, it was because of YouTube that I started to learn C++ coding in a way I hadn't done before. Soon after I was programming electronics and getting into robotics.

A whole new world opened up to me by the fact that I could do a video about anything that caught my interest. I could do video documentation of my research and put it out for others to try and possibly give feedback.

It is also good for coming back to past projects and visually refreshing what I did on a project.

Project after Project and video after video was uploaded to YouTube. I thought my videos were doing well. But, they could have been doing a lot better.

Starting out, editing my videos through Movie Maker was amazing. I was learning how to cut the frames and edit out mistakes. But, I outgrew Movie Maker quickly. I went through and tested a lot of video editing software. I was focused on getting all that right. Eventually I did, but......

My Major mistake was not learning how to market my videos. That hurt my Channel growth in the worst kind of way.

Every time I would try to learn about marketing for my YouTube Channel, I just could not find a way.

Well, I found the way. I am passing it on to you. Most YouTube Creators are making the same mistakes I made. This book is my way of helping others past the problems I had.

For some, their videos are great and they figure they don't need to do all the extra. To that, I ask: Imagine how much better your videos and channel growth would be if you did do the extra?

This book is for those that want to "make perfect" their craft as a YouTube Creator. I am going to give you tips and ideas to put your YouTube videos in the best light possible.

By the way Subscribe to my YouTube Channel at: Ebonygeek45

https://www.youtube.com/ebonygeek45

Also, a lot of the research here is straight from Tippy. Subscribe to her YouTube Channel at: Tippys Thoughts – Tippys YouTube Tips

https://www.youtube.com/channel/UCZdLD5qe6ab3YNopDahDhjA

CHAPTER 1: LETS TALK ABOUT WORKING WITH YOUTUBE

It is fairly easy to start a YouTube Channel. That is not where people have problems. It will be assumed that you already have your YouTube Channel started. You've posted at least one YouTube video and published it.

Common Problems YouTube Creators Have

That is where most YouTube Creator's problems start. Right after uploading your YouTube video you're faced with the:

1. Titles

2. Descriptions

3. Tags

4. Thumbnails

5. etc

What do YouTube Creators do?

They do only what is required to publish the video.

How do I know?

Because that is what I did. My mind would go blank. I knew what my video was about. But, I was in vlogging mode. (Vlogging mean video Blog, or pretty much videos).

Mistake 1 :

> Add a Title without researching the Title

Mistake 2

> Add very little or no description

Mistake 3

> Add very little or no tags

Mistake 4

> Use the Thumbnail that YouTube Created.

Mistake 5

> Skipped over the rest.

Does this sound like what you do with your YouTube Videos?

If so, you are not alone. This is what a lot of YouTube Creators do. It hurts your YouTube Channel. You may get a lot of views, you may even get subscribers.

But you will do a lot better if you work with YouTube and the setup they have.

Why?

Because your Title, description, tags, Thumbnails, etc are all things that YouTube provide you to position your video to work with their algorithm.

By ignoring these things or just adding as little generic information as possible, you are not giving YouTube enough information to slot your YouTube Video right.

What that means is Your YouTube videos will not be readily available for your Target Audience to find you on YouTube. If it does by some chance land in the correct search, it will not be ranked high enough to be discovered. That is, unless you are very lucky and have a viral video. Even if your video is viral, it still won't get the maximum exposure it could have.

The YouTube Creators that know how to work with YouTube have an advantage over YouTube Creators that don't.

Knowing how to work with YouTube is extremely beneficial for New YouTube Creators especially. The reason for this is new YouTube Creators don't have any kind of ranking. They have to work their way up to it. As your YouTube Channel grow, YouTube will add additional help for your YouTube Videos.

YouTube Creators that have experience also need the added benefits of knowing how to work with YouTube in order to jump start their video ranking.

Tippy and I have done a number of video reviews. We have also checked out videos from small YouTube Creators to large YouTube Creators. What we realized is that MOST YouTube Creators are making these mistakes over and over again.

Here is where we come in to help. We are going to take you through it step by step. We are going to show you what we have learned in our research. By the time you finish this book you will know how to market your channel on YouTube.

We suggest that you keep track of your results before you start following the steps we are going to walk you through, and track the results after you've followed the step. We guarantee you will see an improvement.

Read through this book first to understand how this big Marketing Puzzle for YouTube fits together. Then try it again using the examples to get a better understanding. Next try it using the information for your own videos.

Use this book as a tool to improve the visability of your YouTube Videos to find your targeted audience on YouTube.

Again, subscribe to ebonygeek45 and Tippys Thoughts - Tippys YouTube Tips if this book helps you. It will help us continue the research we do to bring you more valuable information.

So, let's get started.

On to chapter 2 >>>>

Creator Studio Classic – Video Manager

It starts off with Creator Studio Classic. At the time this book is being written, there is the regular Creator Studio Classic, and the Beta Version that will be the new Creator Studio Classic.

For simplicity sake we will be using the regular Creator Studio Classic.. We will just refer to it as Creator Studio shown below in image 1 below.

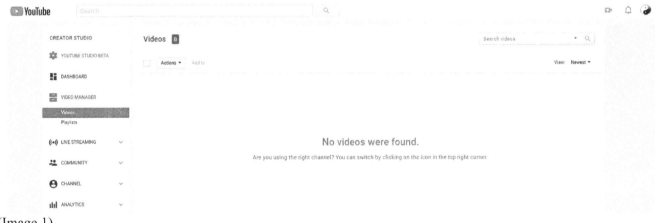

(Image 1)

The example above is a new YouTube Channel. This is what you will see if you are a new YouTube Creator. To catch up with us create your first awesome video and upload it.

For YouTube Creators who already have videos uploaded, You will see your videos where it says No videos were found.

As stated in chapter 1. It is assumed that you have your Channel Created, and at least 1 video uploaded.

We are going to jump right into the thick of it. That is where YouTube Creators start to have problems once they upload their videos.

To get the best out of the steps we are taking you through, you should have a YouTube video that you can work with your own information relevant to your YouTube Video.

My channel Ebonygeek45 is shown here in Image 2 with the many Videos I have uploaded.

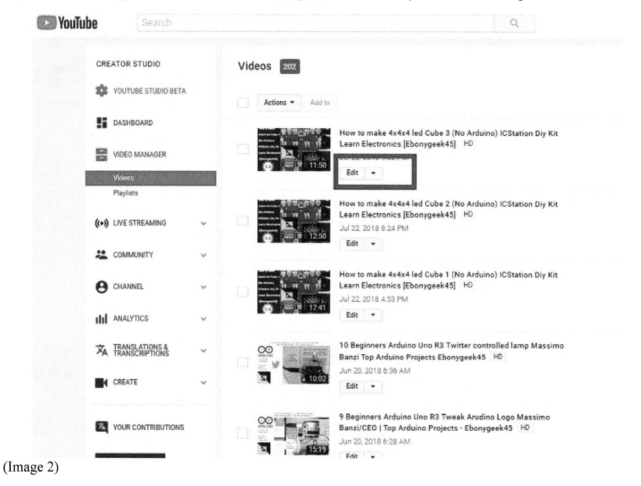

(Image 2)

Pick the video you want to start with and click edit as shown in Image 2.

The example video shown in <u>Image 3</u> is one that was done when I didn't know how to work with YouTube's Video Manager for my YouTube videos.

The video was based on fixing an error dealing with the Eclipse IDE. It is a video that is outdated now. The potential for the video was wasted because the target Audience was not found.

That is why it is extremely important to find your target audience for your YouTube Videos. Especially if it is a video that will only be valid for a certain time These videos you want to get to the people who can use it as soon as possible.

It can save them a lot of time and frustration. They want to find YouTube videos that tell them how to solve a problem or do something. Yet this video was there for them to use, but they could not find it because I did not make it "Search Ready. Don't make the same mistake.

Be smart!! Make your YouTube videos "Search Ready" .

(Image 3)

Let's back up.

When you are creating your video and doing your video editing, you should already be planning out your "YouTube Upload Strategy" .

It is not enough to just upload your video and only do what is required by YouTube to get your video published.

Not to say you can't do just that, but more than likely your video will not be able to compete with other videos. Especially if those other videos are taking advantage of everything YouTube offers to market their videos.

Planning your "YouTube Upload Strategy" while you are creating and editing your video can give you that extra edge.

Take a look at image 3 again keeping in mind that no planning was done for this video when I posted it.

There are 4 areas with blue boxes around them. Those areas are problem areas for this video. There are more, but the few shown is why this video never went to its fullest potential.

YouTube Video Titles – What's in a name??

This is where I would start drawing a blank. My video was made and uploaded. But, how to find a name for my video that people would find interesting. I needed a title that would come up in YouTube's search. Even better if it came up in YouTube Auto-suggest search.

Let's face it, this is about selling your videos to viewers. The wrong name can keep your video from blasting off.

The title needs to do quite a few things:

1. Describe what your video is about.
2. Be relevant as far as the content of your video
3. It needs to be interesting to potential viewers
4. It should entice viewers to click on your video.
5. It must be "Search Ready"

The Title is very important, it must do a lot of things. One of the first things people see is your Title for your video. Your video Thumbnail is also one of the first things people will see for your video. A couple things go into creating just the right Title for your YouTube Video.

What's in a name?? For the Title of your YouTube video there is quite a bit in a name. The last thing you want to do is rush though finding a good title.

Steps to building a YouTube Upload Strategy

Let's start with building a YouTube Upload Strategy. As said before get used to planning out your videos when you are creating and editing your video. For now let's work with what we have.

Planning step 1. Develop out your Title

If you have a title in mind you can start with that. It will change as you work on your tags.

If you are completely drawing a blank for your Title, don't worry about it. We will come back to it.

Even though we have it as step 1, it is something you will keep coming back to.

Stay with me. You will understand more as we go along. I am just outlining the steps for you.

Planning step 2. Finding tags to work for your YouTube Video.

What's in a name??
Answer : Tags

1. Tags (This is the key to make your YouTube videos "Search Ready").
2. Your YouTube Channel Name

I can't stress enough how important it is that you understand. Tags should make up the largest percent of the Title name of your YouTube Video

That is one of the reasons why a title should not just be chosen out of thin air without planning. The key is to bring tags that you researched into your title for your YouTube video. More on this later.

Planning step 3. Custom Thumbnail

Your Thumbnail along with your title is the deciding factor on whether a viewer will choose to click on your video or not.

People Underestimate the power of creating a custom Thumbnail for YouTube videos. Thumbnails are what pull the eye to the title of your YouTube video. YouTube has analytics specifically for measuring the performance of your Thumbnail. That alone should tell you how important thumbnails are to your YouTube video.

Planning step 4. Your YouTube Description

Once you have done the steps above, working with your description should not be hard. It is just a matter of summarizing your video, and bringing your Title and Tags into it where it is appropriate.

That does not mean just adding your Title name and all of your tags.

Tags need to be in understandable sentences when you add them to the description.

Just adding a list of tags to the description one after the other is against YouTube Policy.

What that means is add your title and a summary of your video using tags that will explain your video in easy to read understandable sentences.

You can be creative with your descriptions as well and add other things :

1. Links that can supplement your earnings outside of YouTube
2. Drive traffic to a website
3. list your social media links
4. etc.

You are given more than enough space to use the description of your video to your advantage.

Planning step 5. Add cards for each of your YouTube Videos.

Cards are a way to draw the viewer's eye to something you may want them to notice.

It can be :

- Your own YouTube Videos
- Your own YouTube Videos that are in a playlist
- Another YouTube Channel you feel will help your viewers.
- Donations, if you have a platform to accept them
- Polls that you want to gather information from for some reason
- Links to approved sites

Some of the options above you can use right away and I highly recommend that you do. At least three cards should be added to each of your videos.

Planning step 6 Add End Screens for each of your YouTube Videos

End Screens are similar to cards. The difference is they come up at the end of the video. The goal is to pull the viewer's eye to a call of action before the video ends.

It is highly likely that a viewer who enjoyed your video will choose an End Screen to see more of your videos. Three End Screens should be perfect.

End Screens have the same options as cards with the exception of Donations and Polls. They are also set up slightly different. But you will see later how easy and fast they are to use.

Planning step 7. Add a comment to start your YouTube Videos off

You can be creative with your comment.

You want to add a comment to start your video off. It is much better than leaving your comments blank while waiting for viewers to add comments. This shows that you are willing to engage. If you don't comment on your own videos, why would someone else?

It is up to you to start nurturing engagement with your viewers. Once you get to the point that you are getting more comments than you can handle, others will be happy to handle it for you.

Like and heart your comment. This may entice your viewers to join in. Especially if your comment is good.

Comments allow your viewers to engage with you and others that comment on your video. You want viewers to start conversations about your videos. You want to engage with them as much as possible and comments is how you do that.

Planning step 8. Add your videos to playlist

There are many reasons why you want to add your videos to a playlist.

Think about the music you add to playlist. People make playlist to make it easy to go through music they are interested in..

It is the same for your YouTube videos. Make it easy for your viewers. If they can't or won't click through all your videos, they may be willing to play through a playlist that you have all your video added to.

You don't want to lose them to another YouTube Creator and Channel. Create a playlist so you can direct them through your videos. Especially if you have a series of videos.

Planning step 9. Make sure to blast your new YouTube Video releases in social media.

YouTube Itself is a social media. A lot of people don't realize that. Yes, it is entertainment, research, learning, etc. YouTube is also a social media. Of course you want to engage and interact with your YouTube Viewers on YouTube. That is something you don't want to lose sight of.

You also want to blast your YouTube Video out on other social medias.

Personally, I find that Twitter has brought traffic to my YouTube Channel better than the others. But, that may be because Twitter is the one I prefer.

So use social media to bring viewers to your YouTube Channel.

We now have our YouTube Upload strategy.

Using this strategy will solve every problem area that we saw in Image 3 and more. Each step is briefly explained here.

The chapters ahead is where you will learn how to work with the steps.

CHAPTER 3: ALL ABOUT TITLES AND TAGS

The Nuts and Bolts of it

Planning step 1: Develop out your Title and Planning step 2: Finding tags to work for your YouTube Video, has to be done together.

Again, you have to have tags to make titles for your YouTube video that is "Search Ready". Tags are keywords in the YouTube world. When a viewer search for something on YouTube, it is searching through tags to bring up what the viewer wants.

There are a couple sayings that apply here:

1. The right tool for the right job.
2. People have their own ways to do the same thing.
3. If you're going to do something, do it right

These sayings come into play because, there are a lot of online tools you can use. There are so many that it is confusing to people which ones to use.

I am going to share with you some of the ones I use. They work for me, and if they work for me they are sure to work for you.

This is my way to work with YouTube. As you grow and start working with this strategy, you are sure to find your own way. There is nothing wrong with experimenting. Find what works for you. The strategy I am outlining and explaining to you will work with any kind of YouTube video and subject.

So, if you are going to make YouTube Videos, why not start them off the right way. That way you can adjust and build from there.

Of course we will be using YouTube itself with these tools because it just makes sense.

Keywords Everywhere

The first tool is called Keywords Everywhere. It can be used with Google Chrome or Mozilla FireFox. It is fairly easy to install. You may need to get the API key for it and just add it to the application. The link is below.

https://keywordseverywhere.com

It is a Browser extension for Firefox and Chrome.

Keywords Everywhere eliminates the need to switch between your keyword tool and Google Keyword Planner. That is if you did. For those that was not using the keyword tool and Google Keyword Planner, this is a simpler way to do keyword(tags) research.

Keywords Everywhere is perfect for exactly what we will be doing. It is super simple to install.

Simply click on either 'Install for Chrome' or 'Install for Firefox' in accordance to your current browser preference as shown in Image A below.

If you find it is not working once you have it installed, just add the free API.

Don't let the API name scare you off. They make it so simple to add a 10 year old can do it.

From the home page, click GET FREE API KEY as shown in Image A below.

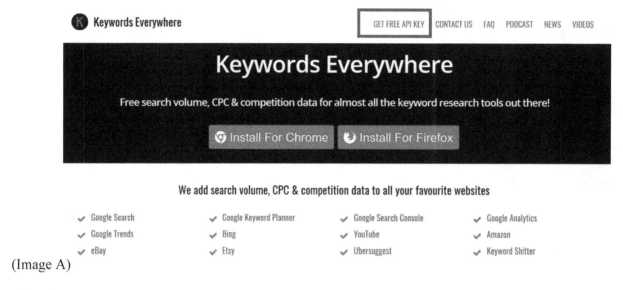

(Image A)

Give the email you want the API to be emailed to > Agree to the terms and > Click the Email me API Key Button as shown in Image B below.

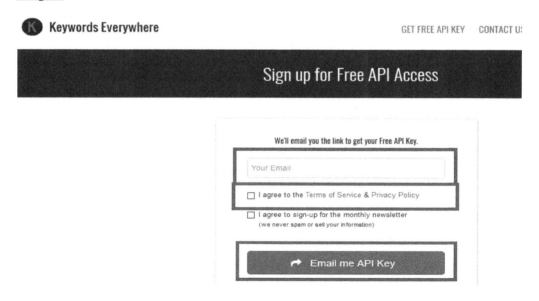

(Image B)

The email should arrive within 10 minutes. If you don't see it check your emails spam and trash folder. Sometimes, it is confused as unwanted email.

Once you have clicked into the email sent from Keywords everywhere, You will see something like Image C Below.

In case you have not received it in 10 minutes, please check your Spam/Junk folder. If you do not find it there, y

Open the email and click the link in it

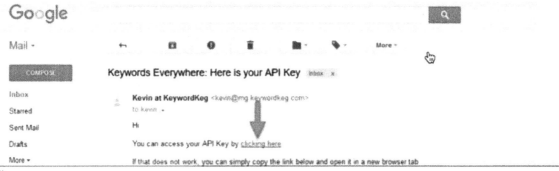

(Image C)

Click the link to get your API key > Copy It.

Go to the browser that you installed Keywords everywhere on.

When you Click the Icon for Keywords Everywhere at the top of your browser, you will see where you can update it's settings as shown in Image D below.

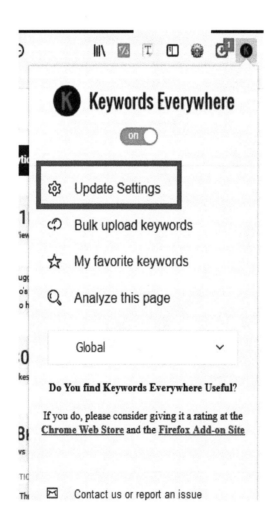

(Image D)

Click Update Settings

Right away you will see where to paste your API key as shown in (Image E).

Click the blue validate button and you will have a working version of Keywords Everywhere.

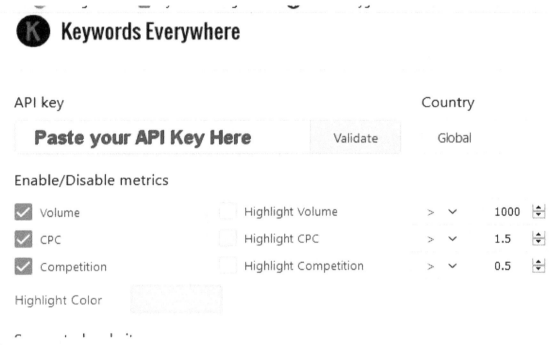

(Image E)

For now this is the only tool you need. It is free, and it is going to help in a big way.

There are other settings that can make Keywords Everywhere, even simpler for you.

For now I would say get familiar with it, then if you feel you want to change the settings go ahead.

We will specifically be using Volume(which is search volume).

Keywords Everywhere is a great tool and I would suggest getting to know it more whenever you can.

Let's get back to YouTube.

(Image 4)

Image 4 above should be familiar to you(Disregard my video info). This is an example of the Title and Tags field.

1. Your title field
2. Your tag field

We will start with 2 your tag field. I will stress often that tags are very important. Don't ignore them!!

First, I will show you how to find the tags we will need. Remember, what I am showing can be done for any subject for a YouTube Video. What I show you is examples. You would add information for your video following the example given. The examples work for all YouTube Video Subjects.

The example will be for a Video on Twitter Advanced Search.

Twitter Advanced Search may be of use to you, I have done a video on it.

https://youtu.be/yYEvncyvVhg

Finding those good "Search Ready" Tags

How do we start out working with Tags?

Let's work with the little information relating to the subject. Below are simple keywords I feel is relevant to the video.

1. Twitter
2. Advanced
3. Search
4. SEO

That's easy, right? It doesn't take a lot of thought to start on your way to working on finding good tags. Now let's let the YouTube search engine do some of the work for us.

You don't have to have a video uploaded to YouTube at this point. That is what makes this strategy good for planning before you even have a YouTube Video. You can find tags and see what the results are. Which is good for figuring out if you should make a video on the subject before you make the video.

Planning out your video and having powerful tags before you make the video is extremely useful. When you know good powerful tags before you create your video, you can make sure to say those tags in your video. YouTube will pick up on the fact that you said your tags in your YouTube Video and it will add to the relevance.

Don't worry if you created your video already. You can use your tags in the description. But, make sure it is in a valid form. That means in an understandable sentence. You can not just list them with no real purpose. That is a no no with YouTube.

So, let's get started

Type Twitter into the search box slowly.

What did you notice?

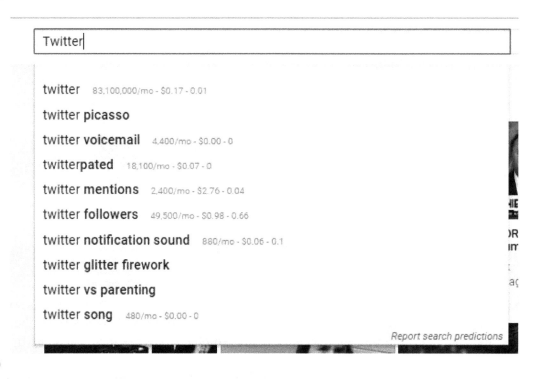

(Image 5)

The first thing you should notice is the Auto Suggest functionality of YouTube Search. Most of the time you don't even have to type out the whole thing before it shows the results in the drop down.

We typed "Twitter" As shown in <u>Image 5</u>. YouTube Auto Suggest kicks in with trending tags you can use.

Yes, these are tags that come up right away.

These are the tags you want to use if it is relevant to your video. Do not use the ones that are not related to your video. You don't want to mislead your viewers with tags that have nothing to do with your YouTube Video.

Try it for the subject for your YouTube Video

For the example subject, nothing is relevant.

No worries, we would just check the other 3.

But, we add them to Twitter to drill down to our videos subject. Remember to type slowly to see if there are auto suggestions you can grab. For example. The next one will be "Twitter Advanced".

I am showing valid results with "Twitter Adv".

(Image 6)

At this point you should have keywords everywhere working for YouTube.

Keywords Everywhere is very important because it will show you the search volume of the tags you see. You are looking for the search volume per month.

For instance (back to Image 6) for "twitter adv" :

Twitter Advanced Search 135,000/mo - $1.08 - 0

Twitter Advanced Search is the YouTube search result. The numbers after Twitter Advanced Search is the search volume per month(that is what we want). The dollar amount Keywords Everywhere is giving you is good to know, but not something we are using.

135,000 searches a month is very good. But it may also mean that the competition for your video to rank can be too high.

You would use it because it is the subject of the video.. In this case you would not worry about the competition.

When the tag is 1 to 2 words, it is a short-tail keyword by my standards. In most cases when using a short-tail keyword the competition is going to be high. For example "Twitter" in Image 5.

Each tag will have the search volume next to it. We are not using the dollar amounts. Just the search volume per month. We want keywords to use as tags that have a high enough search volume per month. The minimum search volume you should be looking for is 4,000/mo especially if you are a new YouTube Channel.

As I said the reason you are typing the keyword that will become the YouTube tag slowly is to pick up other keywords that are trending in the auto-suggest.

From Image 6 we have a few that are relevant, but only Twitter advanced meets the minimum from above. It is the only one we add to our list.

Let's continue on. "Twitter Search" is next on our list. You would do it the same way we did "Twitter" and "Twitter Advanced".

So far we have 3

1.   Twitter Advanced Search
2.   Twitter Advanced
3.   Twitter Search

Twitter SEO Did not meet the minimum.

We can also do variations of the keywords that will become our tags like below.

1. Advanced Twitter Search
2. Advanced Twitter
3. Search Twitter

They also meet the minimum and are good for us to use.

Go ahead and try it out. Keep an eye on the monthly search volume from keywords everywhere.

Remember, you have a limit to how many tags you can use. There is no point in wasting your tags on low volume tags.

Just type in relevant keywords to see what you can find.

This is just practice so you understand the concept when using the example subject.

Try it for the subject for your YouTube Video

It should be easy to figure out how it works:

1. You are typing in relevant keywords in the YouTube search bar
2. Then you are choosing from the drop down relevant keywords that can be used as tags
3. You are making sure they are at the least 4,000/mo for the search volume with Keywords Everywhere
4. You are keeping a list of tags that good

Knowing how to get the keywords that will become tags can help you in **many** ways.

We have a list of keywords with potential. Now we need to check the competition for these keywords.

For that we are going to use another tool.

Actually, there are two tools that you can use according to which one you like the most. The names and links are below.

VidIQ
https://vidiq.com/#_1_bg

TubeBuddy
https://www.tubebuddy.com/Ebonygeek45

Both these tools do mostly the same thing. The reason why they were not brought up before is because, for the free version you have to know how to get your keywords that will become tags.

If it is in your budget to use the paid versions, I would suggest VidIQ Boost. It is very powerful and can save you time.

We will go with VidIQ the free version for now. Again, it is fairly easy to install.

Once you have it installed, at first glance you may be turned off from it because there is a lot going on. You will see a lot of VidIQ Icons and graphs they provide you, all of this is going to help you. These tools are very good, especially now that we know how to find keywords for the tags.

First off you want your YouTube Channel name to get to the point where it is ranked with YouTube. You want it to have a good rank. One way to do this is to make sure it is in your Title, Description, and Tags.

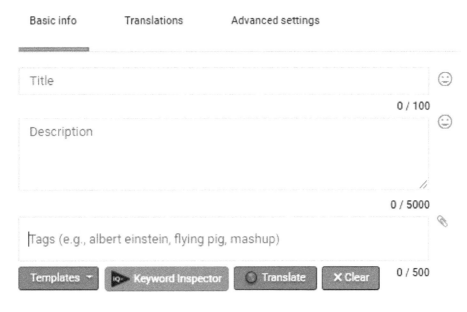

(Image 7)

Let's start with the tags.

Image 7 is showing the Title, Description, and tags for YouTube. The Blue and Gray buttons are for VidIQ. If you do not see them make sure you installed VidIQ correctly.

My Channel name is Ebonygeek45 and that is going to be the first tag I add. Your Channel name should be the first tag you add for all your YouTube Videos for your YouTube Channel. That is how you build up it's rank within YouTube.

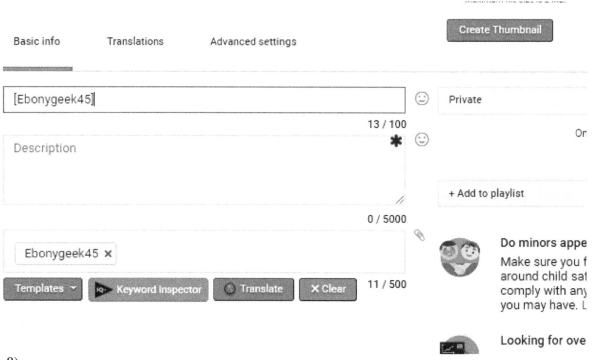

(Image 8)

Image 8 shows Ebonygeek45 being added to my tags. It is my Channel name so I also added it to my Title.

Later Ebonygeek45 will be added to my description.

This is the Beginning of adding tags to my title to make them work the best they can for me. Remember you are adding your channel name the same as you see me adding mine in Image 7.

Now, we were talking about search volume which you should know how to get for keywords. We also want to know what is the competition for these keywords.

The tag for my Channel name can be clicked on to show some valuable information. So click on your channel name in the tags and we will go over what it shows.

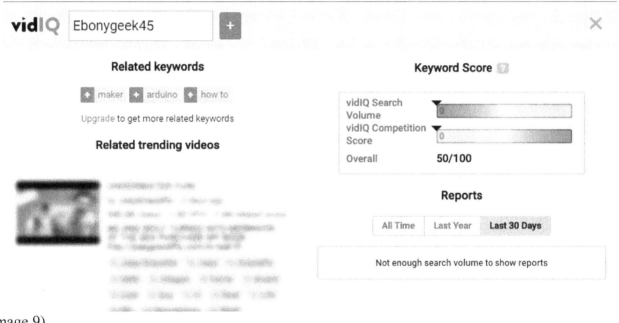

(Image 9)

Another window will pop up with additional information for my tag for my YouTube Channel name.

Related keywords will give you a few suggestions. If they are relevant you can use them. But make sure to click on them first and check for the Keyword Score. The Keyword Score is the second thing you should see. It shows the Search Volume and Competition Score for VidIQ.

For your Channel name it will start off low and as you add it to more videos it will go higher. So, you want to make sure that you add it to all your videos for your channel.

Related trending videos are going to be blurred out for the free version of VidIQ.

That is also why you will only have a few Related keywords for VidIQ.

That is why I showed you how to get keywords in YouTube with the help of Keywords Everywhere. As long as you follow those instructions you will be able to find more than enough tags for your YouTube videos.

Free is always good to me. But, if you can afford to buy the Boost or Pro version of VidIQ and you can justify the cost, go ahead. It will be a time saver for you. For now we are going with the free.

You will also see reports which would be a graph to show you how the tag is doing. As shown for my Channel Tag, there is "Not enough search volume to show reports". But you will see this graph showing results later.

Back to keyword Score for my channel name Image 9. You see both the Search Volume and Competition Score are at 0. This is not surprising for my Channel's tags. It will be low until it is built up.

Back to the keywords we researched earlier. The first set of keywords we came up with was :

1. Twitter Advanced Search
2. Twitter Advanced
3. Twitter Search

Let's get a little practice in. We Type Twitter Advanced Search in the tags box for the example video.

Try it for the subject for your YouTube Video

Everything you do for the example video can be done for your YouTube videos on any Subject.

To get used to the strategy try the example video first to see how the example work. Then try it with your own YouTube Video Subject.

(Image 10)

Notice that VidIQ also makes auto-suggestions shown in Image 10 above. This is another way to get tags if you see new ones you can add.

Once you have it added as a tag click on it to find the Competition Score.

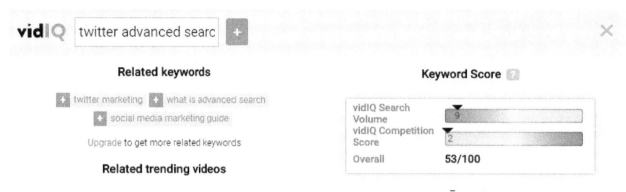

(Image 11)

Time to put on your Thinking cap.

What we are seeing in Image 11 is Search volume in the Red. Ideally, we want to see it in the green. But, remember we already check the search volume with keywords everywhere. We know that the search volume is higher than 4,000/mo. In fact, it is 135,000 shown in Image 6. We are good on the Search volume.

Competition Score is what we want now. It is in the green on the side we like, which is far from the yellow. This is a very good competition score. We will definitely take it. "Twitter Advanced Search" is a good tag. In fact, it may be the one we use when putting the Title together.

See how easy that is??
How this work is :

1. We are looking for competition score
2. The further it is from the yellow the better
3. If it is close to the Yellow, the competition score is too high and we don't want to use that tag.

Go ahead and check the other 2 on the list, then come back here. It is easy, do it the same way as we just did "Twitter Advanced Search".

Keep in mind that the results may change for you. The images shown at the time of writing of this book is accurate for this time.

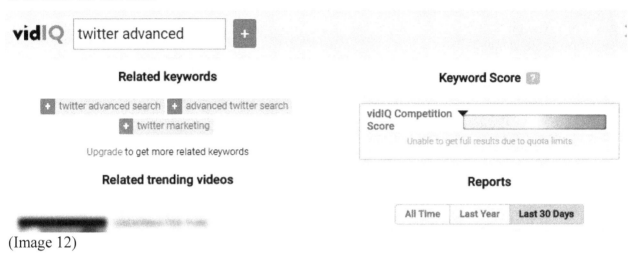

(Image 12)

At times you will see results showing like Image 12 for "Twitter Advanced". This is fine because it is showing the competition is low. We already know that the search volume is good. So we will use "Twitter Advanced" too.

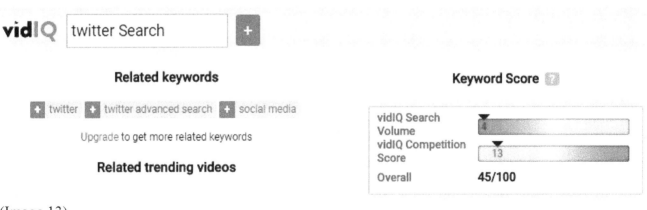

(Image 13)

"Twitter search" is also showing good. We will take it. For our first three examples the Competition Score is nicely in the green

There are times when it will be on the other end of the spectrum and show in the red. That means that the competition score is high.

There are a few reasons why you would ignore the high competition score:

1.   It is the specific name of the subject of your YouTube Video.
2.   It is the name of your YouTube Channel.
3.   It is a tag that I call a staple tag which will be high.
4.   It is a short-tail pulled from your tags

A staple tag is a high volume keyword/tag that users are known to use that comes first in YouTube auto suggest.

For example :

1. Where does
2. What is

A short-tail pulled from your tags is when you break up a long tail tag you have researched. You would use the most important words and leave out words like :
- the
- it
- to

For example an easy one is:
"Twitter Advanced Search"
The short-tails you would pull out is:

1. Twitter
2. Advanced
3. Search

As you can see they are pulled from my long tail tag. They will be high in competition, but since it is pulled from the long-tail tag we will ignore the high competition. The other reason is they are highly relevant to my YouTube Video.

For long-tail keywords you don't want to use tags that have high competition.

Only use short-tail keywords for tags that you pulled out of long tail keywords that were good.

High Competition Score means there is a lot of YouTube Creators using the keyword as a tag. So many that you would have little chance being seen through that keyword as a tag. You don't want to be in the red.

Low Competition Score is what we are looking for. That means you want it to be in the green as far away from yellow as possible.

The Yellow you can think of as a barrier that you don't want to go past for Competition Score. Definitely not in the red. Again, you would only ignore the competition score for the reasons stated above.

Let's go back to "Twitter Advanced Search" shown below in Image 14.

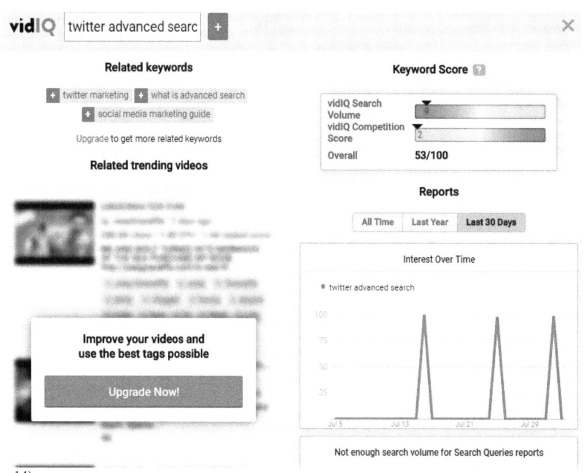

(Image 14)

Image 14 is also showing graphical results in Reports in the form of the chart. It is a visual way to see how good the keyword did over time by the last 30 days, the last year, and all time.

That is a good way to investigate as to when the keyword go high and over time what it does. For instance for games, I would think the keyword would go high on the release date of the game. If you are inclined to investigate the keywords for the subject of your videos, you may be able to broadcast the best time to make videos.

Below reports you will see related queries as shown above in Image 14. It is saying there is "Not enough search volume for Search Queries reports. That's OK. Sometimes it will show sometimes it won't.

For now get some extra practice with the other 3 tags we researched.
Try it for the subject for your YouTube Video

For the example video they were :

1. Advanced Twitter Search
2. Advanced Twitter
3. Search Twitter

If you saw the competition score in the green that is what we have too.

Here is another tip to find keywords to use as tags. Let's use "Twitter Search Advanced".

We know that we will get auto-suggestions in the search bar for YouTube. When you type the tag into the search bar. You can scroll down to the YouTube videos that come up and see the tags that YouTube Creators are using for their YouTube Videos.

If it is not showing up like shown below for Image 15...

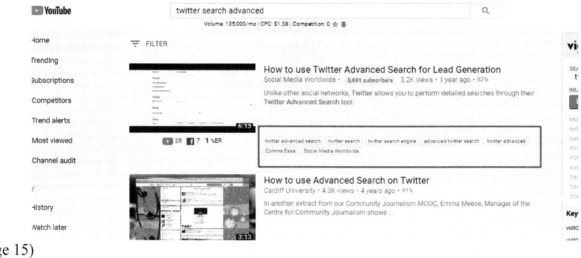

(Image 15)

You can click into the video and see their tags as shown in <u>Image 16</u>. .

(Image 16)

This is really good for finding more tags for your YouTube videos if they are relevant for your video.

Remember that these are tags other people are using. You want to choose the best ones you can. So make sure you check their search volume and competition score.

Finding your tags this way will give you more tag ideas then you need. It is just a matter of putting in the time to get the best ones. They are there all you have to do is check the search volume and the competition score. The time you put into it can pay off.

Here I followed the instructions above to get the best tags for my video. They are below. I try to get it as close to 500 as possible.

I use a combination of short-tail and long-tail tags.

They all work together through search.

Here is what I got copied straight out of YouTube's tags..

> ebonygeek45,Twitter Advanced Search,Twitter Advanced,Twitter Search,Advanced Twitter Search,Advanced Twitter,Search Twitter,Twitter,Advanced,Search,Twitter how to use,Twitter UserName,Search Twitter hashtags,how to use,how to,UserName,hashtags,hashtag,User Name,Advanced Search,Twitter target keywords,target keywords,Keyword search,Keywords,social media for beginners,social media Marketing Strategy,Social Media tips,social media,Beginners,Tips

Tags for YouTube are not like hashtags. Add them normally with spaces. Commas will separate your tags.

Other than the many ways I have explained to find tags for Your YouTube videos, there are many other ways to go about it. The more you work with tags, the more you will find better ways.

Tags are very important. They should not be ignored. Even if you haven't been using tags and your YouTube Videos have done well. They would do a lot better if you use them.

For simplicity :

1. Add them to your tags

2. Click on each one and check the competition.

3. For VidIQ the search volume may show low on some tags. By using keywords everywhere as shown above, you will know if it has the volume you are looking for (minimum 4,000/mo). So, even if the Search volume is shown in the red for VidIQ, if Keywords everywhere shows it above the minimum, It is OK to use. Especially for new YouTube Channels starting out, or small YouTube Channels.

4. Keep checking for more keywords and tags as you are going with the YouTube Search and the other ways shown in this chapter.

5. Add the good keywords as tags in you tags field.

6. The limit is 500 and you should be able to find them for any subject with the processes explained above.

Chapter Summary :

At this point you should be able to find tags that you can rank for on YouTube.

That's a good start and should get you all the tags you need. Good tags that can work for you.

If for some reason you come up short (Which you shouldn't, with practice it will become easier and easier.)

You can use the google search engine the same way we showed above to use YouTube search with auto suggestion. That should get you the tags you need. But, it is best to use YouTube Search for auto suggestion first.

Also, for those that have already completed their videos, you can review your video and listen for keywords for tags. If you're saying something a lot on the video that can be broken down into tags, make sure to use them.

You want to fill your tags up as close to the 500 limit as you can.

The hardest part to tags is finding the right ones. Knowing how will cut out a lot of confusion and make it simple for you. This chapter gives many examples and ways to work with tags. Let's go on to the next thing we want to focus on.

CHAPTER 4: CREATING GREAT SEARCH READY TITLES

Have you wondered why we started with the tags?

It is simple. We are going to use the tags to create powerful "Search Ready" Titles.

Just like with the tags, the first thing I am adding is my YouTube Channel Name. I am using it as my tag identifier(You can have more than 1 tag identifier in your tags, try to use only one in your Title.). It is short and should work fine for the title.

If you have a long channel name you should create a shortened version that you use as a tag in all your videos. The reason is you need one that can be added to your title. But, does not take up too much space in your Title.

I always add it in square brackets as shown in Image 17 below.

(Image 17)

The next thing to do is decide which one of the tags you want to use in your Title. That is why all your tags need to be relevant to your video. You will use your tags in other ways.

You want to use the ones with the best search volume and competition score. Because you should have pulled short-tail's from long-tails, those short tails will also be in the Title.

Understanding Things And Some Review

Once you download your video to YouTube, you can leave it as just adding the required information to publish your video. That is was a lot of YouTube Creators do.

It is to your advantage to find every way you can to make your YouTube Video stand out. YouTube offers many ways to optimize your YouTube videos. You can do this with YouTube Metadata.

Metadata for YouTube is :

1.   Title
2.   Description
3.   Tags
4.   Thumbnails
5.   Playlist
6.   End Screens
7.   Cards
8.   Comments

In other words, by my standards, it is everything you do after you upload your videos within YouTube Video Manager.

It is completely up to you as a YouTube Creator to be as detailed with this information as you want. You can then step up your efforts through your choice of Social Media if you like.

It can be time consuming when you first start out. As you do more and get used to working with YouTube's Metadata for your video, it becomes easier.

Starting off with tags is a part of the process I created. It is not the beginning of the process. The beginning is when you create your video. Again tags should be kept in mind when you create your videos.

We went over tags in Chapter 3. If you followed along with Chapter 3 you should be able to find great tags for any subject of video you have.

We will look through these tags to create our Title.

The reason for using tags to develop the title for the YouTube video is simple.

1.   You've researched the tags already
2.   You know the search volume for your tags are good
3.   The competition for the tags ranking on YouTube is good
4.   The tags are relevant and tailor made to your YouTube Video.

Developing the YouTube Video Title

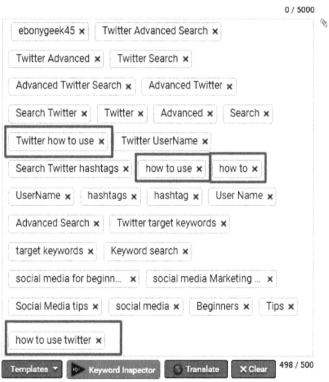

(Image 18)

In my tags I have what I call staple tags which are explained in Chapter 3. They are shown in <u>Image 18</u> above:

"How to".... Is always a good staple tag and good for the title. If you can find a tag with good Search Volume and Competition score, it should be a part of the title. But, choose the best because the title has a limit.

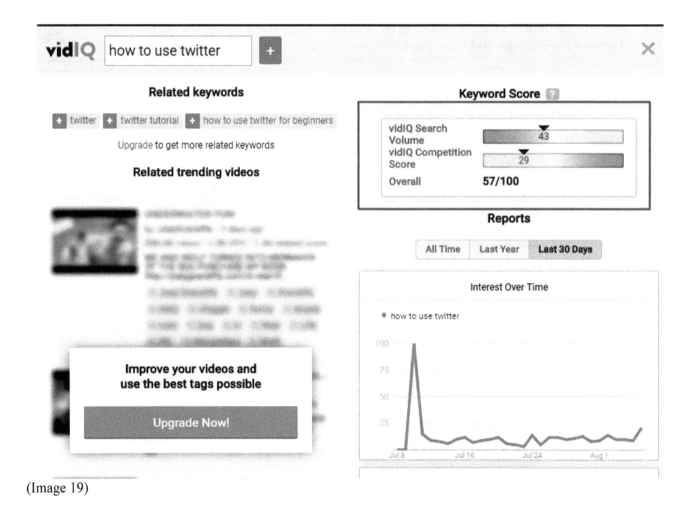

(Image 19)

Image 19 and Image 20 is showing a good "how to" tag with the scores we are looking for.

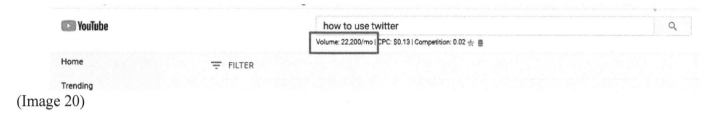

(Image 20)

We are going to add it to our Title as seen below in Image 21.

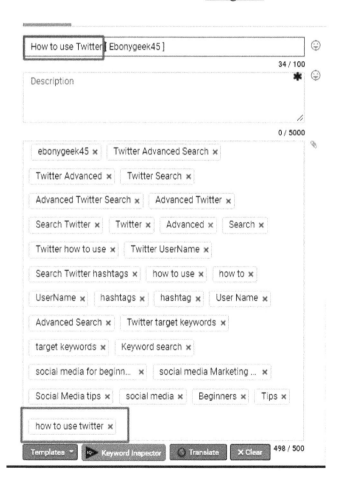

(Image 21)

Take a look at Image 22 :

Notice how the Title for the YouTube Video is made up of all tags. There are only two small words in the title that is not in the tags. They are used to make the Title sound like a Title.

Also, the Title is more "Search Ready" by adding more of the tags we researched.

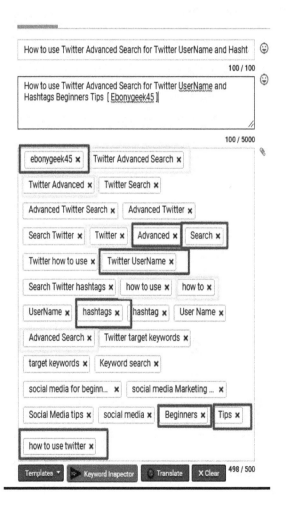

(Image 22)

Blue is showing tags used in the Title. Yellow is showing tags that indirectly fit in the title also.

The Title is 100 characters. It is right at the character limit for YouTube Titles.

The title is easy to understand and readable everyday English. The Title is filled with tags, with the exception of the one word "for".

This is very important because it means that the title of the video is completely "Search Ready" with great tags.

In Summary :

The Title and the Thumbnail are very Important to your YouTube video. Think of them as the window and doorway to your YouTube Video.

For this reason, it is very important to put in the time to make them work for your YouTube Video.

We are still following the strategy outlined at the beginning of this book. We have our tags, and we just developed our Title.

That title is developed with the use of tags. Finding the best tags possible will in turn make a great "Search Ready" Title. Your creativeness in how you piece the tags together in your Title can make it enticing for the viewer to click on. Hitting on the right balance will be very good for your YouTube Videos. Now on to Thumbnails in the next chapter.

CHAPTER 5: YOUTUBE CUSTOM THUMBNAILS

Custom Thumbnails are also a creative process to your YouTube Videos. There are a lot of different ways to go about it.

The one thing you don't want to do is use the default Thumbnail YouTube automatically supplies for your video.

Some of them look really good. But, this is your chance to visually present your video to viewers. You can do a lot better job than YouTube's program does.

Viewers are going to pick the YouTube video that captures their eye. Thumbnails are great for that.

My big mistake on my channel was to use my brand for each Thumbnail.

Don't make the same mistake.

1. It doesn't show the viewer what the video is about. That means the Title has to do all the work for your video.

2. You may be proud of your brand. I felt viewers getting used to seeing my brand would mean they would click on my videos. This does not work for big companies and it didn't work for me.

3. In a way it shows laziness by slapping the same image on each video. This was not true in my case. But, it is the lazy way. If you don't take the time to create a visual for your video as a preview, don't be surprised if the viewers do not watch your video. Why? Because someone else will take the time. They will be happy to take your potential viewers.

Thumbnails are very - and may I stress **very** important. You want to create the best Thumbnail you can for your video.

Start paying attention to other YouTube Creators Thumbnails and how they look.

Pay attention to the thumbnails you yourself tend to click on.

How you create your Thumbnail will be according to what software you use and how well you know it. Just like with your videos it is a part of your creative process.

Some tips are :

1. Find the image software that works best for you. Personally, I like gimp. It allows for layering that keeps my process organized. You can use others like Photoshop or Canva . It is all a matter of preference. Whichever one you choose, make sure it can do what you need to create great Thumbnails.

2. You want to make sure to use vibrant colors that will stand out from YouTube's colors and overshadow other Thumbnails . This is so that your Thumbnail stands out. You don't want it to blend in with all the others on YouTube or to blend in with YouTube's Theme.

3. Use your Judgment. If you see nothing but Bright, vibrant colored Thumbnails for a Tag, You may want to rethink your strategy. One way is to do a screen shot of a really good point in your video. Use that as Your Thumbnail. Of course, adding key points in your title and anything else to make your Thumbnail pop. What this means is take a look at the Thumbnails for your tags. Decide what will make your Thumbnail Stand out from the others and do it.

4. Add the best part of your Title to your Thumbnail. Remember Your Thumbnail is small. The whole Title will be tricky to fit on your Thumbnails. It can be done. But try using enticing click attractive parts of your Title for your thumbnails.

5. When you have the portion of your Title you will use, make the text as big as you can in an attractive way. It needs to be visible without blocking any images you want to show for your Thumbnail.

6. Your Images should be what you know as "click-baity". Don't get me wrong. You want it to be relevant to your video. But you want it to be something viewers want to click on as well.

7. Don't overthink it.

8. Some people add images of themselves in a great pose. Some people use images of something interesting in their video. Some make use of eye catching backgrounds. Use whatever work for that particular video.

9. Just let your Creativity flow. Look at your Thumbnail. Is it something you would click on? Are the images and text clear? Is it enticing to the eye?

10. Don't get stuck on one theme for a Thumbnail. You should always check Thumbnails for videos under the tags you want to rank in. Then create a Thumbnail that will beat all the others(at least do your best to.) That means Your Thumbnails should not look alike if you are giving them all your special attention.

Mastering Thumbnails can show you a jump in your views. Why?

Because no one wants to click on a boring thumbnail, unless you have an irresistible Title for your video. Mostly it is the Thumbnail that catches the eye and lead someone to click on your video to see if it is what they are looking for.

For example, here is how the Thumbnail looks for the YouTube Video I am working on. It is showing up on one of the tags It was ranking for.. shown in Image 23 below.

Social Media for Beginners Tutorial | Twitter Advanced Search SEO and hashtags | Ebonygeek45

Ebonygeek45 · 36 views · 4 months ago

Social Media for Beginners Tutorial | Twitter Advanced Search SEO | Ebonygeek45 Twitter Advanced Search - Finding the best ...

(Image 23)

Right from the start, we see some problems :

- The black edges are wrong
- The description is repeating the title
- The Title is not as visible as it should be for the Thumbnail image
- The images are OK, but could be better
- There is no need to have two of the same images
- Since it is Twitter, There should be a Twitter Icon

The thumbnail showing in Image 23 is not popping. It is trying, but is not great.

At the same time it is better than the default YouTube Thumbnail.

To give a brief example of how I create my Thumbnails :

- Using my PrtSc button (It means print screen and is on the top row of your keyboard over the + symbol). I am going to play the video in full screen mode. When it gets to a point that I want for the Thumbnail, I will just press PrtSc. That captures the Screen at the point in the video I want. Pretty much like the Thumbnail for Image 23 started out.

- You can also use your snip tool, or a video editing software that captures stills.

- It depends on how you want your Thumbnail to look. I will use the screen capture as my background. You can also create a nice background. It is all in how you want to do it.

- Once I have captured the screen, all I have to do is paste it in Gimp as shown in Image 24 below on a transparent background.

- The width and the height for your Thumbnail should be 1920 x 1200.

(Image 24)

In gimp the image from the screen capture can be:

- Added to a background
- Moved around
- Layers with text and pictures can be added to it
- Be touched up
- Colors can be sharpened or dulled

In other words you can really work with the image until you are happy with it for your Thumbnail.

I am told Photoshop is a lot like gimp and vice versa. If that is what you like, by all means use it.

Canva is an online image software that is free. It is another option for you to decide on.

I know Gimp best and can vouch for it. Although it has a learning curve that is not so hard if you look up YouTube Videos for what you want to do.

Again, this is not a tutorial on using gimp. Gimp is mostly trial and error. It is a free image software. It is worth your time to learn. There is a lot that Gimp has to offer.

If Gimp is a little much for you, Others like Canva. It is free also. The learning curve is not so stiff.

I stress it is worth learning how to make great Thumbnails.

Image 25 below is the new Thumbnail created for my video.

(Image 25)

Notice the improvements for the new Thumbnail :

- The images are now more relevant to my video
- The text is more pronounce and visible for the Thumbnail
- Black borders are gone for the Thumbnail.
- Twitter Icon is added, as well as my brand for my YouTube Channel.

- More Focus to the Twitter Feature the video is about.

Next I add it to my YouTube video :

It is as simple as:
1. Click Custom Thumbnail
2. Navigate to the Thumbnail where ever you saved it
3. Select the Image.

How to use Twitter Advanced Search for Twitter UserName and Hashtags Beginners Tips [Ebonygeek45]

Ebonygeek45 · 40 views · 4 months ago

Finding the best keywords for Twitter hashtags in Twitter. The search bar is good but, Twitter's Advanced Search feature is better.

(Image 26)

Here is how the New Thumbnail displays for Image 26 above. You are free to judge the difference.

Looking at Image 26 :

1. We see the Image
2. Title of the video
3. Below the Title is: My Channel name
4. Views at the time
5. How long the video has been published on YouTube.
6. Under the Channel Name, Views, and Published Time Frame, is the part of the description that is displayed.

Something you should notice about the portion of the description displayed:

The first 1½ lines of your description is very Important. This is what will show for your search results like shown in Image 26 above.

Add a very **brief Summary** or the information that you want to show first and foremost. Use that first 1½ line of your description to its best potential...

Don't waste it. The biggest waste is not to use it at all.

You do want to add the Title of your video in your description. But not in that key placement. If you do add it on the first 1½ lines it will just repeat the Title that is already there. It makes no sense to repeat the title one on top of the other.

It took me a minute to figure out that mistake.

If you compare Image 23 to Image 26 you will see the difference. Image 26 is better and the one I would click on.

That is the importance of adding good Thumbnails, making sure you have a good "Search Ready" Title, and making sure that you first 1½ lines of the description is good. That is what your viewers will see when they search out one of the great tags you researched to rank on.

It all ties together. If you do it just right, you will see a jump in your views and definitely in your YouTube Video impressions.

In Summary:

Thumbnails are a part of your creative process. There are many ways to make a great Thumbnail.

It is in your best interest to find the software you like the best to make custom Thumbnails for Your YouTube Video.

Do not skip over the Thumbnails. That is a big mistake because Thumbnails are one of the first things viewers see about your video. You want to make them attractive to a viewer. Make them stand out as much as possible.

Again, the software I like to make my Thumbnails is Gimp. Others have told me that Photoshop and Canva is also good for making Thumbnails.

Take your time with it and enjoy the creative process. The more you work on improving your Thumbnails the easier it will get.

Now that we got that out of the way we are going to go on to Descriptions in the next chapter.

CHAPTER 6: YOUTUBE DESCRIPTIONS

YouTube Descriptions are something that I really struggled with.

- What do you add?

- Am I adding to much?

- Am I adding to little?

- Do people even pay attention to the descriptions?

The questions went on and on as I overthought it.

In the end I came to realize that overthinking it was exactly the wrong thing to do.

Add to your description what you want to add to it.

What I learned was again. You want to summarize your YouTube video briefly in the first 1½ lines.

The reason you want to do that is the first 1½ lines of the YouTube Description is the sweet spot. It will go with your video where ever you post it. For instance Twitter, Facebook, and YouTube Itself.

You don't want to give everything away in that first 1½ lines of your video. Otherwise, why would people click on your video. Just a brief teaser summary to let them know what the video is about, and entice them to watch your video.

After the first 1½ lines of the description You can do what you like:

1. A more detailed summary of the video without giving too much away. Making sure to add tags wherever possible and relevant. Do not add tags just for the sake of adding them. Structure your sentences to use tags without overdoing it to the point your sentences don't make sense.

2. The Title of your video(Which should always be added). It is a good practice and is OK to paste it as it is in the description. Just don't add it in the first 1 ½ lines(sweet spot) of your description or it will repeat. No need for repeating.

3. You can add links to other social networks like Twitter, Facebook, etc

4. If you have affiliate links you can add them.

5. If you have other YouTube Channels or videos you would like to shout out you can do that.

As you can see there is quite a bit you can add to your description.

As long as you keep it organized and well spaced there should be no problem.

Take a look at other YouTube Creators descriptions to see if someone sets up their description in a way you liked.

That is another way to get ideas on how to work with your YouTube Descriptions.

Try to make sure there are no errors.

Also keep your description up to date and accurate.

YouTube gives you 5000 characters in which to make a good description for your videos.

That is plenty of space to get your description added they way you want.

I find that I hardly ever go over half of that limit.

If you need the 5000 characters use it. If you don't, no worries.

As long as you get in the details you want, making sure to add the teaser summary for the first 1 ½ sweet spot, and add the title of the video after it, you are good to go.

Below is what I had for the description for the video we have been working on :

Finding the best keywords for Twitter hashtags in Twitter. The search bar is good, but Twitter's Advanced Search feature is better.

Watch this video to see how to access it.

The Twitter Advance Search Feature is a great way to locate useful hashtags and User Names. You can target keywords to search more accurately through Twitter.

You can drop this in your social media tips tool-bag. Every little bit counts when you are trying to find your target audience on Twitter. Having a Social Media Marketing Strategy can really help your YouTube Videos gain more traffic.

Please subscribe to this channel to know when more videos are posted. Comment and share this video.

How to use Twitter Advanced Search for Twitter UserName and Hashtags Beginners Tips [Ebonygeek45]

Link for Twitters Advanced Search Feature:
https://twitter.com/search-advanced

Ebonygeek45 videos focus on bring more people into electronics and programming. It is the wave of the future.

If you are new to Arduino, the kit below will give you a great amount of components to experiment with. It also has an instruction book.

Hot Tip!! VidIQ is a great YouTube Channel tool that can save you time get it at the link below :
https://vidiq.com/#_l_bg

Watch the videos all the way through so you don't miss anything.

Please Subscribe to this Channel to be updated on more great Arduino Tutorials. Click the link below
www.youtube.com/ebonygeek45?sub_confirmation=1

Comment, like, and share.

If you have any hot tips for Ebonygeek45, comment below.

Subscribe and Network with Ebonygeek45 on YouTube at the link below
https://www.youtube.com/ebonygeek45

Follow Ebonygeek45 on Twitter at the link below
https://www.twitter.com/ebonygeek

Friend Ebonygeek45 on Facebook at the link below
https://www.facebook.com/ebonygeek45

Network with Ebonygeek45 on Google+ at the link below
http://bit.ly/Ebonygeek45GooglePlus

Ebonygeek45 Shop offers Ebonygeek45 E-books at Straight from the Author Discount Prices at the link below
http://bit.ly/Ebonygeek45Shop

Get yourself and/or your kids involved in the world of programming small electronics. The door to robotics and diy electronic projects.

Kids do well in science fairs and learning how to troubleshoot their way to problems, when they learn how to work with Arduino Uno.

Start them off with a beginners series book. Click the link below to buy the E-book at a very special price.
http://bit.ly/EbonygeekEbookSale

Tippys Thoughts - Tippys YouTube Tips

If you are a YouTube Creator, check out Tippys Thoughts - Tippys YouTube Tips. You may be able to use something that will improve your YouTube Growth.

https://www.youtube.com/channel/UCZdLD5qe6ab3YNopDahDhjA

DISCLAIMER: This video and description may contain affiliate links, which means that if you click on one of the product links, I'll receive a small commission. This helps support the channel and allows us to continue to make videos like this. Thank you for the support!

Hot Tip!! TubeBuddy can help you grow and market your YouTube Channel get it at the link below:

https://www.tubebuddy.com/Ebonygeek45

As you can see I added quite a bit to my description. I used it to market my videos, my social media, affiliate links, and to ask for much needed subscriptions and comments. It only came up to 2,913 characters.

The link to go directly to Twitter Advanced Search was also added in my description.

Do what feel is right concerning your descriptions.

People do scan through the description from time to time to get more on your video. If you really found someone with a like mind, they will want more information to contact you. Or see more videos. Even purchase something from your affiliate links.

Your description is the place to add all that extra information. If you can supply information to your viewers rather than them googling it....all the better.

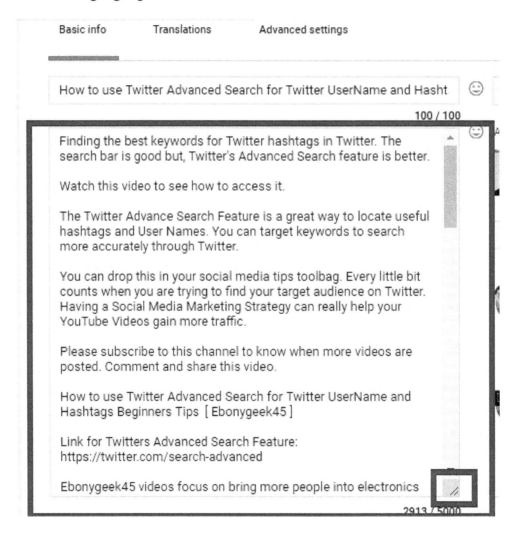

(Image F)

Image F is showing where I added my Description.

When you add your Description, the box you add it to may seem small.

Notice the...

at the bottom corner of <u>Image F</u>.

If you click on it, you can drag the description box down to see it better as you draft your description.

Neatness counts. Make it attractive and evenly spaced. Do not bunch it all together.

People like well organized descriptions.

In Summary.

Creating good YouTube descriptions is pretty simple, don't overthink your description.

Use it to supply whatever information you want to your viewers.

As long as you get in the details you want, making sure to add the teaser summary for the first 1½ lines (sweet spot), tags where appropriate, and add the title of the video after it, you are good to go.

See how simple that was!?

On to the next chapter.

CHAPTER 7: CARDS AND ENDSCREENS

You can now take a breather, but you're not finished yet.

Understand that what has been explained so far is something you may not catch on to right away, some will.

This is mostly a case of the more you practice the better you will get. The better you get, the better it will be for your YouTube Videos and YouTube Channel. It will get easier and faster as you go.

There are a few more things to do to improve your YouTube Video's chances.

You have done the most important work. The rest is very easy and quick to do.

So easy and quick that you want to make sure to do them.

YouTube Cards

As pointed out in Chapter 2 :

Cards are a way to draw the viewer's eye to something you may want them to notice.
It can be :

- Your own YouTube Videos
- Your own YouTube Videos that are in a playlist
- Another YouTube Channel you feel will help your viewers.
- Donations, if you have a platform to accept them
- Polls that you want to gather information from for some reason
- Links to approve sites

Below in Image 28 the card is for my video on how to make a Led cube.

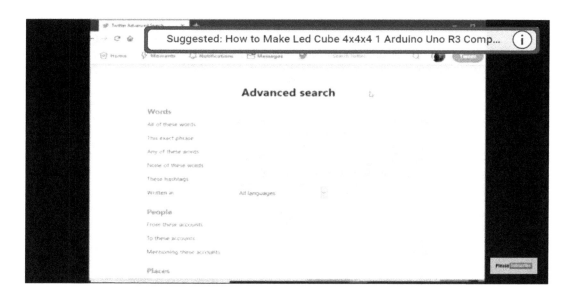

(Image 28)

The card pops up and stays up for a moment. In some cases, your viewer may be interested in what the card is showing. When they click on it, they go to whatever the card is about.

In this way you can keep the viewer engaged in the cards that you create to keep them on your YouTube Content.

When you click on cards shown in Image 29.....

(Image 29)

You will come to the screen in <u>Image 30</u>.....

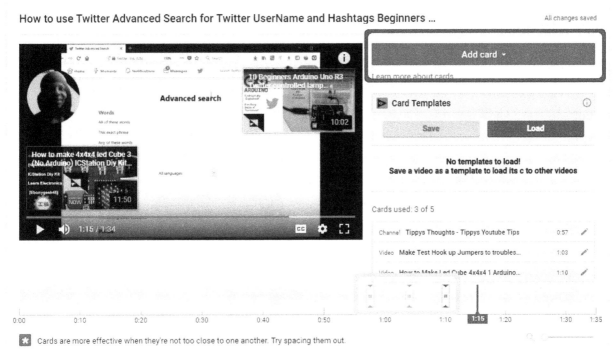

(Image 30)

Make sure you place your cards strategically.

For instance, if you place them at the beginning of your YouTube Video, the viewer will not get a chance to view the video they clicked on.

If you place the card at the end of the video, it will have to compete with your end screens(More on that next).

I place my cards right before the end screens as shown in Image 30 above. End screens will show for the last 20 seconds of your YouTube video.

Click on Add Card and the options shown in Image 31 will display.

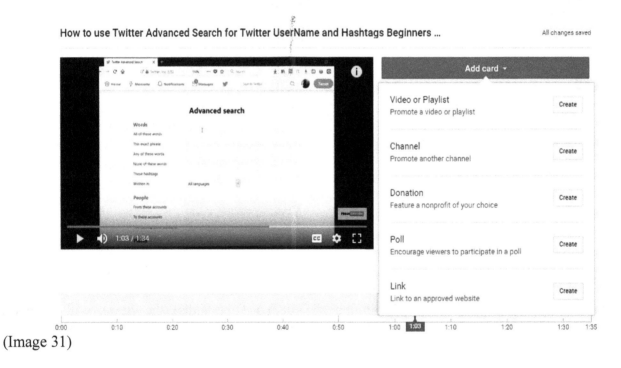

(Image 31)

Pick the options that you want for your card and choose Create.

Follow along with the card that prompts for the particular type of prompt you want to create.

Personally, here are the cards I like to add:

- a Video
- a Playlist
- a Channel for another YouTube Creator I support

In turn the YouTube Creator for the Channel I support also add a card for me. This is a way you can support other YouTube Creators and they do the same for you.

When you first start off there may be options you can't use yet. As your YouTube Channel grows, you will be able to use other options.

Cards are a way to steer your viewers to the options you set up.

You can :

- Do a poll
- Go to a YouTube Video
- Go to a YouTube Channel
- Go to a playlist
- Or Even go to a website page

It is up to you to give your viewers other options within your YouTube Video. Options that keep them engaged in a way you direct.

That can lead to a lot of other possibilities for you to Engage further with your YouTube Viewers.

YouTube End Screens

End Screens are similar to Cards.

The difference is that the End Screens will automatically come up at the end of your YouTube Videos for the last 20 seconds.

But, Cards can be placed where ever you want within your YouTube video.

In a way End Screens are easier because with Cards you have to carefully decide where to place them. If you place cards to early your viewer may not get a chance to see the video they were viewing if they click on the card. You don't have to worry about that with End Screens.

Just click on End Screen as shown in Image 29 above and the options in Image 32 below will display.

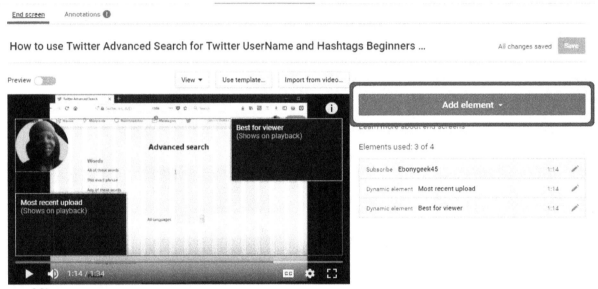

(Image 32)

Click on the Add Element button.

This will "Overlay" these elements on your YouTube Video 20 seconds from the end.

If you want to see how it will look you can simply click the Preview Option over your video shown above in Image 32.

Note:

Annotation is no longer valid for YouTube, It is outdated.

YouTube dropped it so you can't use it even if you want to.

It is meant for cards to take its place because cards work well with cell phones and tablets, it is said that Annotations did not..

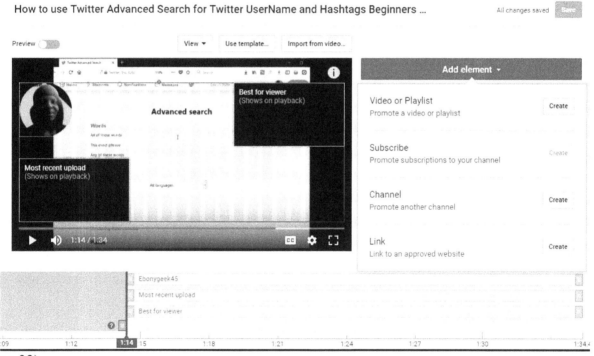

(Image 33)

Here on end screens you have 4 options. You don't have "Donations" or "Poll" like you have with cards, but you do have "Subscribe". I use "Subscribe" for all my YouTube Videos. So the option for "Subscribe" for your end screen is very important.

The subscribe will show your icon as seen in Image 33 above. The other 2 elements showing in Image 33 above are "Best for viewers" and "Most recent upload". Those are the three that I use for my end screens.

To get "Best for viewers" and "Most recent upload" click on Create for Videos and playlist see Image 34.

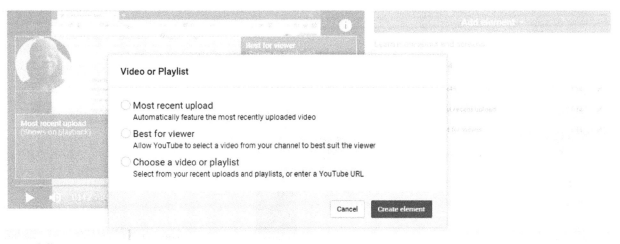

(Image 34)

You can only add one element at a time.

Most recent upload is fairly simple to understand. It is my first choice of elements to use because it will automatically update and display my most recent upload.

"Best for viewer" is the other element I use. Instead of trying to figure out which video or playlist I want to add, in this case I let YouTube Choose it. Since it is my YouTube Videos it will choose from I am fine with that.

Once you pick the option you want, all you have to do is click the Create element button and you are done.

I use 3 elements for my end screens :

1. Subscriber
2. Most Recent Upload
3. Best For Viewer

That's all there is to end screens. Just another tool YouTube offers to allow you to engage with your YouTube viewers further after they viewed your video.

In Summary :

Cards are very simple to create. They allow to engage with your YouTube viewer further.

They are so quick and easy to add that you want to make sure to use them. Do not overlook the advantages it gives you to engage further with your YouTube viewer.

End Screens also allow you to engage with your YouTube viewers further. They are a lot like cards, but they display in a different way.

End Screens captures your viewer's eye just as your video is ending. If your YouTube Viewer enjoys your YouTube video they will be quick to click on the end screens you offer.

That is a much better offer than your YouTube viewer coming to the end of your video and there are no options for them to continue on with your videos, or however else you want to direct them.

The Morale of this chapter : Make Sure To Use Cards And End Screens.

CHAPTER 8: PLAYLISTS AND COMMENTS

Time to wrap up it up with Playlists and Comments.

You should use create playlists for your YouTube videos for a number of reasons :

- If you have a series of videos
- For all your videos
- For related videos
- To keep your videos organized

It is like having a playlist for music on your iPod or mobile phone.

The biggest advantage is that it sets your videos on auto play for whatever videos you have in the playlist. Your YouTube viewer can choose a playlist. The playlist will automatically play each video you added to the playlist. They can even set it to repeat.

Why is that something you should be concerned with?

Because if you have a YouTube viewer that choose your playlist, they will watch your video all the way through for each video in your playlist.

If your playlist is playing for that viewer, it will continue to play and maybe even repeat(If they have it set to repeat).

Sometimes people will walk away from their computer and if they leave your playlist playing, that will still count for views for you.

I know that we want them to view the videos themselves, but if they forget and keep it running all the better for you. In most cases, if they like your videos they will come back to where they left off and continue with your playlist.

Playlist are good for your YouTube Channel.

Viewers that watch through your playlist are you loyal viewers and more than likely the ones that will engage with you the most.

Playlist are simple to add. You should have at least one playlist that you create and add all your videos to. Then you should have playlist for series videos, related videos, and however else you want to organize your videos into playlist.

Click on playlist as shown in Image 35.

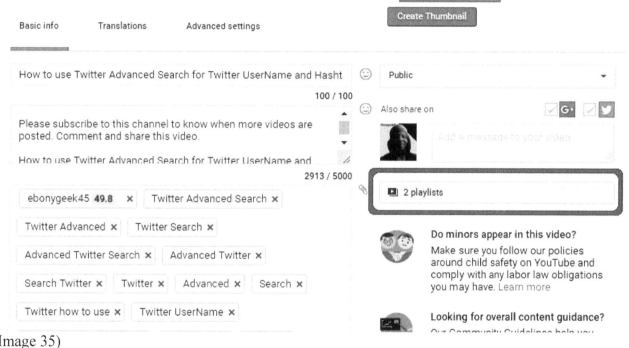

(Image 35)

As I explained before Image 35 above is showing that this video is in 2 playlists

1. A playlist that I add all my YouTube Videos to.
2. A playlist with related videos on the same subject of this video

You want to have a minimum of 3 videos for each playlist. Having just 1 or 2 videos in a playlist kind of defeats the point for playlists.

That is why the playlist with all your videos added to it is a good idea. If you are new it should not be hard to get to the point where you do have 3 videos for your first playlist. If you are a seasoned YouTube Creator you should not have a problem creating playlist to organize your YouTube Videos into.

Once you click on playlist, you will see a list of the playlist you have as shown below in Image 36.

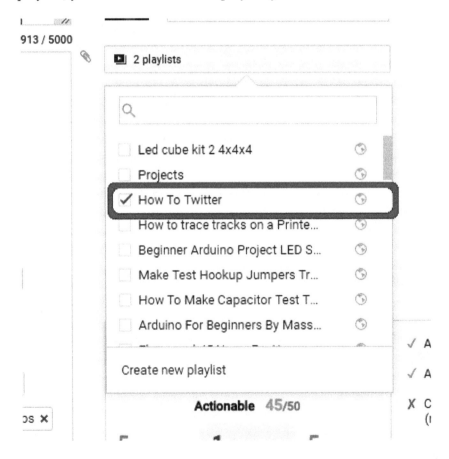

(Image 36)

If you have playlist created and know which one you want your YouTube Video to be in, it is as simple as clicking the box to check it.

If you want to Create a new playlist for your YouTube Video, Click Create New Playlist as shown in Image 36 and Image 37 will show.

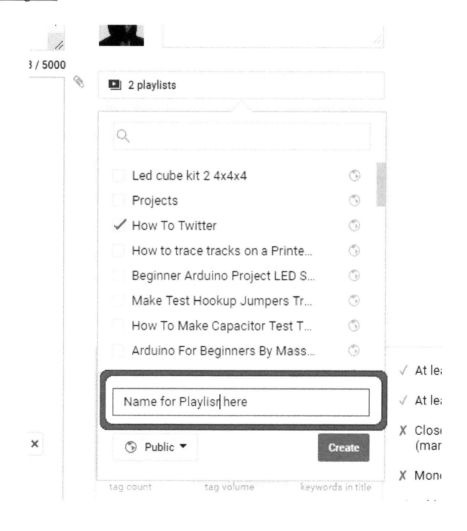

(Image 37)

Add whatever name you want for the playlist in the box. In Image 37 above I added "Name for Playlisr here". Of course that is not the name I want for a playlist. It is just an example to show you where the name you choose for your playlist can be added.

Once you add the name for your playlist Click the Create button. Image 38 below shows what happens once you click create.

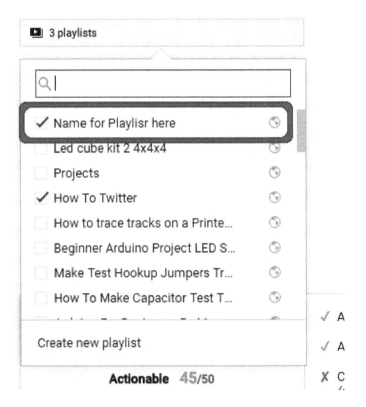

(Image 38)

As you can see in Image 38 above the new playlist is added. I Misspelled it above but you get the idea. The newly created playlist is checked, meaning that My video is added to it. If I decide I don't want it in that playlist all I have to do is click on it to un-check it.

With playlist explained and why you should use them, let's go on to YouTube Comments.

YouTube Comments

I am sure you know what YouTube Comments is. People tend to not bother with it at all unless they get a comment from someone.

Did you know that adding a comment to your videos once you Upload it can help your chances of people commenting on your videos?

The reason for this is because you comments won't look as empty. They see that you may be willing to comment back to them.

For no other reason, it helps your YouTube video itself.

Personally, I like to try to be the first to comment on my videos. There is nothing wrong with it. Image 39 Below shows the comments for this video. The first comment I made for this video is the second one.

When you make your first comment make sure to give it a thumbs up, pin it, and heart it as shown below.

The comment itself is part of the description that I added to my YouTube video at that time.

If YouTube Viewers skip over my video summary in my description, they will see it here in my comments.

My comment below is not pinned as shown in Image 39 below. Once I got my first good comment I pinned it as shown.

2 Comments ☰ SORT BY ▶ | All comment threads (choose filter) ▼ |

Add a public comment...

⚑ Pinned by Ebonygeek45

CoriolisAffectment 2 months ago   1,408 subscribers
Well, that's timely. Thanks for that ebg45. :)

👍 1 👎 💬   REPLY ⧐

Ebonygeek45 3 months ago
Twitter Advanced search is very simple. At the same time has more power than the regular search box. For one thing your search can be more specific, by keywords or exact keywords. You can also search by date. Experiment with it. It is worth your getting to know it

👍 1 👎 💬   REPLY ⧐

(Image 39)

Once you start getting comments from viewers about your YouTube Channel, make sure to give them a thumbs up and heart them. That is if it is a favorable comment.

About YouTube trolls, my advise it to ignore them. Don't let them pull you into any kind of drama that will look bad for your YouTube Channel.

Me myself, I kind of like playing with trolls. But whenever I do I keep a cool head and don't allow them to get to me. My focus with trolls is to make them look as silly as they are, while at the same time killing them with kindness.

If you allow trolls to get you into an insult war, it makes your YouTube Channel look bad. Remember Trolls are trying to get attention by getting others to troll you on your YouTube Channel. Ignoring them don't allow them to do that.

Don't feed the trolls.

Try to respond in words to good comments. This will show up well with YouTube as you are engaging with your YouTube Viewers. It also can lead to good dialog on the subject matter of your YouTube Videos.

YouTube videos with a lot of comments tend to do well. Make sure to show that you welcome comments and will respond. Especially when you are first starting out your YouTube Channel.

In Summary :

Playlists are a way of guiding viewers through your videos. If you have a series of videos or related videos it helps your YouTube viewer stay on track with the flow of your videos.

If you have a Playlist with all your videos in it, your YouTube Viewers may discover one of your videos they like that they didn't know you did. It also gives them the opportunity to play through all your videos.

YouTube viewers that view your playlist are your loyal viewers. You want to provide them with playlist ordered the way you want them to view your videos. It is very frustrating to like a YouTube Creators videos and a series they did, just to have to search for a video in their series to get to the next video.

Make it easy for them. Once you find loyal YouTube Viewers do everything you can to keep them, and keep them happy.

Engage with your loyal viewers. If they take the time to comment on your YouTube Videos, comment back to them. YouTube Viewers that find a YouTube Creator they really like become fans of that YouTube Channel. Getting feedback from the YouTube Creator makes them feel good.

For those that comment to you about something in your video they didn't understand, it shows you in a good light to comment back to them with an explanation.

There are all kinds of engagement that will help your YouTube Channel grow. You want to make sure to take advantage of anything you can to cut through YouTube Competition.

If you show you are engaging on your YouTube channel and in your comments, others will tend to want to join in and engage as well.

That is what you want to help your YouTube Channel grow.

CHAPTER 9: YOUTUBE AND SOCIAL MEDIA

We have gone through a strategy to use what YouTube provides you in Creator Studio's Video Manager.

The importance of YouTube Comments and engaging with your YouTube Viewers has been explained.

There are many other ways you can work with your YouTube Videos and Channel.

Make sure to keep an eye on :

Tippys Thoughts – Tippys YouTube Tips
and
Ebonygeek45

...on YouTube for other ways to improve and/or learn new things.

Please, subscribe to our YouTube Channels. We welcome comments, suggestions, and feedback. We also support YouTube Creators that Support us. We're in this together, let's become a community.

Up until this point we focused on what to do to give your YouTube Video the best chances to cut through the huge competition on YouTube itself working with Video Manager and Comments.

You can take it further with Social Media.

Social Media for your YouTube Channel would mean writing another book because there is so much involved, but we are including this Chapter because it is very important.

If you are into a particular Social Media platform, make sure to post your YouTube videos to it. Seek out others. Not just in YouTube, but for the subject of the videos you post on YouTube.

In my opinion Twitter is the easiest to break into. Don't get me wrong, it does take research and a good deal of work to get results, but it is worth learning.

There are many Social Media Platforms according to which you like best. There is :

- Twitter
- Facebook
- Google+
- Reddit
- Instagram
- Pinterest
- Tinder
- etc etc

If you have a working understanding of any of the Social Media's, that is a good way to bring traffic to your YouTube Channel and Videos.

If you have a website or blog, make sure to provide links to your YouTube Channel and videos and vice versa. That is another way to get traffic to your YouTube Channel and Videos.

Don't forget to join forums and communities related to the subject of your YouTube Channel and Videos and link to your YouTube Channel and Videos.

Keep an eye on YouTube analytics to see where traffic is coming from. YouTube Analytics is also something to pay attention to. By using it you can figure out what outside sources(meaning social media) are bringing traffic to your YouTube Channel.

Just like YouTube, Social Media is meant to be "Social". That means socializing with others on that particular platform.

For example... Twitter has all kinds of ways to socialize with those you follow and who follow you.

Engagement is very important and you do that by socializing.

You will hear a lot about how to get more followers and so on. But, you want to get followers that are interested in what you are interested in. That means your Target Audience Just like with YouTube.

Once you start getting followers and you start following people... socialize, ask questions, post new YouTube video releases, ask what people think about it. In other words communicate with people.

Another way to think about it is make it your "Think Tank". That means where you can get ideas and bounce ideas off others for your YouTube Channel or whatever.

When others take a look at your Twitter Account(or whatever Social Media you are using) they will see it is engaging and they will want to join in on the threads and comments.

They may even follow your links to your YouTube Videos and watch them.

There are a lot of tips and tricks to Twitter(I know Twitter best.) That is why I am using it as an example.

Catch me on Twitter and let me know about other Social Media's and how to break into and work with them for YouTube. Let's start some Social Media Conversations that will pull others in that we can socialize with. Remember YouTube it a Social Media too. We want to Socialize on YouTube as well.

I stress. When others see you have a flowing dialog for your YouTube Videos, they will join in and socialize too. Be open to that and respond back. People see it as a treat when a YouTube Creator responds to their comments. They are more likely to become loyal YouTube followers for you.

Social Media is very powerful. You can use it to get in touch with like minded people. My Twitter account would be focused on finding and socializing with :

For Ebonygeek45

- People interested in making things with small electronics and programming them.
- People who use Arduino and more specifically the Arduino Uno R3
- C++ Programmers
- Makers and Tinkers
- Woodworkers and Craftsmen
- YouTube Creators
- People who like Marvel(MCU) comics and movies

- People who like DC(DCU) comics and movies
- People who play any of the Castlevania Video Games and old school Atari Games
- People who are interested in Technology and how it got started
- People who like and are involved with YouTube and Computer Technologies
- E-book and Book writers
- Inventors in the making
- Specifically women that are interested and involved with small electronics, Robotics, and the programming of them. Doesn't matter whether you are a beginner or more advanced(because I was told that as a black female involved in all these things, I am rare. So, I am looking for others.).
- etc, etc, geeky stuff, etc

For Tippy

- YouTube Creators
- YouTube Video Editing and Planning
- People who like Marvel(MCU) comics and movies
- People who like DC(DCU) comics and movies
- People who play any of the Castlevania Video Games and old school Atari Games
- People who like and are involved with YouTube and Computer Technologies
- E-book and Book writers

As you can see some of mine and Tippys interest cross over(we have some of the same interest.). If you look through our subscribers on our YouTube Channels, you will see that we share some of the same subscribers. It is the same for other subscribers. That is called networking. The more we build up our network the more successful we will become. That is where we would socialize with each other.

Tippy and I collaborate on her videos based on our shared interest. I voice a good deal of her videos to help her make them better.

Collaborating with other YouTube Creators is very important. Also, working with sponsors that help you out in some way. Maybe if Tippy see something she knows I like, she would Retweet it or message me about it and vice versa. I have collaborated with a number of YouTube Creators and Sponsors. This is something Tippy and I am open to. It helps you grow your YouTube Channel. Some of these collaborations came straight from Twitter followers or Facebook friends..

Tippy and I would comment and like each others threads where we find something we are interested in that we both want to talk about.

Others would see these threads and possibly join in.

This is how you build up the engagement and "Socialize". This is the same for Facebook.

With these Social Media's you can't just open an account, then leave it at that, or open an account and seek out just anyone. Then just hope that it will do well.

You have to seek out and "Socialize" with others with your same interest. That is how you build a following in Social Media.

When you are first starting out you may grab onto anyone. But, as your Social Media account grows, you can be more selective and targeted.

It is really a process and like I said, I get the most results from Twitter.

If you are just starting out, my links are below. Network with me. Then remember to engage. Let's Socialize with each other and start building up a YouTube Creators Community.

If you have questions about this book follow Ebonygeek45 and Tippy on Twitter and ask those questions. If you like something let us know. If you have ideas for us post it.

If you are into Social Media and can give us a boost or Tips and Tricks let us know. We want to get better with the other Social Media's where it involves bringing traffic to our YouTube Channels. We will then get that information out to others. It is about exchanging information to help others and ourselves.

What better YouTube Community can there be?

Below we have listed our Social Media links we are involved with. You are more than welcomed to join us :

Ebonygeek45

Subscibe to Ebonygeek45
www.youtube.com/ebonygeek45?sub_confirmation=1

Follow Ebonygeek45 On Twitter
https://twitter.com/ebonygeek/

Friend Ebonygeek45 On Facebook
https://www.facebook.com/ebonygeek45/

Network with Ebonygeek45 on Google+
https://plus.google.com/u/0/110923536756316224427

Tippys Thoughts - Tippys YouTube Tips

Subscibe to Tippys Thoughts - Tippys YouTube Tips
www.youtube.com/channel/UCZdLD5qe6ab3YNopDahDhjA?sub_confirmation=1

Follow Tippys Thoughts - Tippys YouTube Tips On Twitter
https://www.twitter.com/under1k45

Friend Tippys Thoughts - Tippys YouTube Tips On Facebook
https://www.facebook.com/YSY-Tippys-Thoughts-650156695375861

Network with Tippys Thoughts - Tippys YouTube Tips on Google+
https://plus.google.com/u/0/b/109137937540538064412

Network, Socialize, and engage with us..

In Summary.

Social Media can be very good for your YouTube Channel growth. It takes patience and the willingness to learn how to make it work for you.

Understand that YouTube Itself is a Social Media. It's just that most of the socializing is going on in the comments of your YouTube Video.

The key is to :

- Find your target audience, seek out others with your same interest.
- "Socialize" on Social Media.
- Ask questions and visit others profiles to see if something is useful, than comment and like.
- If you can answer questions do so, that may lead to others seeking you out.
- Link to your YouTube Videos and Channel.
- When you post images or videos on social media, Make sure images and text to your links are clear and look great.
- Collaborate with others with the same interest as you have.

Again, the Social Media topic is huge. I hope that this Chapter helps you.

I stress and remember that YouTube itself is a social media. Don't forget that. YouTube is changing more and more to create ways for YouTube creators to engage easier with YouTube viewers that like their YouTube Channel. Make sure to keep up with YouTube.

Above all, even if you don't decide to extend your YouTube Channel and Videos to social media, have fun and enjoy the experience.

CHAPTER 10: YOUR YOUTUBE CUSTOM METADATA IMPROVES YOUR YOUTUBE CHANNEL

Most of the strategy that was laid out in this book was hard learned. It is one of those cases of "I wish I would have known all this when I started my YouTube Channel".

But with years come experience and improvement.

The creative process is fun and exciting and you get that rush every time you upload your YouTube Videos.

"This will be the one to jump-start my YouTube Channel" You hope.

But you have to know how to work with YouTube's Metadata. Even if you have a great YouTube Channel with great YouTube Videos, and a huge base of subscribers.

Just think how much better it will be if you just work with the Metadata for each and every YouTube Video you have.

You can't be too successful so it is worth doing.

Remember Metadata is the:
1. Title
2. Description
3. Tags
4. Thumbnails
5. Playlist
6. End Screens
7. Cards
8. Comments

In other words, by my standards, it is everything you do after you upload your videos within YouTube Video Manager.

Adding this information where YouTube has it set up to be added helps YouTube position and work with your YouTube Video.

When you don't use what YouTube offers by:

- not adding the information,
- leaving it blank,
- or just adding anything,

…..You are not giving YouTube the best chance to work with your YouTube video.

Your YouTube Video won't be easily found, seen, or displayed.

YouTube offers a platform for creative people to broadcast themselves out to the public. Anyone can start a YouTube Channel. All it takes is a Smart phone or other form of camera, video editing software, and headsets with a microphone or a more advanced microphone.

For this reason YouTube has grown and exploded since they started. The bigger they get, the more they tighten their reigns on monetization and options YouTube creators can take advantage of.

There was a time that all you had to do was post videos to get monetization privileges, and have the ads run on your videos to make you money.

YouTube has gotten more serious about it. Now you have to earn the right for monetization privileges. That means you have to show you can get subscriptions for your YouTube Videos, and maintain views to your videos.

You can still start your YouTube Channel, but your YouTube Channel need to be productive if you want to make money from YouTube.

But some people aren't in it for the money. They are in it to be heard. They are into it to share something they are proud of. It can be a new dance step, an opinion about something that happened, something they made, etc etc.

It is said if you want to know how to do something, YouTube it. More than likely there is a video that has been made to show you how to do it.

Because of the huge amount of videos on YouTube about any and everything, it is hard to gain a following. The reason for that is competition. Everyone wants their videos to go viral. Everyone wants to be a YouTube Star.

Yet, a lot of people don't know what to do past uploading their YouTube video. A lot of people do only what is required to get their YouTube Video published.

That may have been enough when YouTube first started out. But, in 2018 doing what everyone else is doing is just putting you at the end of the line. At the end of the line, your videos will not get the views that are needed and you will never get to the goals you have for YouTube.

In some cases, people get lucky, but those are rare cases.

This book attempts to give you a strategy to cut through the competition and place your YouTube videos in a better position to get noticed and become discovered by your target audience.

If you have great videos and content, the strategies in this book will help your videos reach their potential to help your YouTube Channel grow. Remember, you do have to put in the work to make videos people will want to watch.

Make sure your camera is giving good quality footage. Make sure your microphone is giving good quality audio. Get creative in your video editing and make sure you add B-roll to help explain your videos and enhance them.

Try not to do the umms, ahhs, and filler sounds and words. If you do, make sure to edit them out.

Try to keep your videos moving without having huge chunks of space where either you are not saying anything, or doing anything or both on your videos.

It is your creative process and your work. So make sure your work is polished and the best you can make it.

If you're new and nervous about Starting a YouTube Channel.

Do it.

It is so rewarding. If I can do it anyone can.

If you are generally a shy person, or bad at being in front of crowds, This is the perfect way for you to work on that issue.

Step out of your comfort zone. Seeing and hearing yourself on video can give you clues on how to work out anything with yourself that you find lacking.

There are many reasons to start, get back into, or continue on with a YouTube Channel :

- You have a skill to share that you want others to learn
- You have a voice about any number of issues in the world
- You have a business that you want to promote
- You want to show off videos from vacations and experiences
- You are trying to build a brand or platform for yourself
- You are an artist of some kind and want to display your art
- You want to share your unique personality with the world
- etc etc

YouTube gives you the chance to create your own Channel catered to your interest.

Above all, have fun.

You are your own YouTube star with your own YouTube Channel and that is something to be proud of.

Ebonygeek45 :
https://www.youtube.com/ebonygeek45

I am a YouTube Creator. My YouTube Channel Ebonygeek45 was started 8 years ago. One of the reasons I started my YouTube Channel was to show a friend what I learned teaching myself C++ . At the time I was not someone that was comfortable on video.

That first morning I grabbed a cup of coffee, put on my new microphone headset, fired up my screen capture software, and made my first YouTube Video. Movie Maker was the video editing software I used.

From there I was hooked. The shyness went away and I got comfortable in my skin on video. Movie Maker served its purpose, but I outgrew it and found better video editing software.

As time went by I learned how to improve my videos.

Friends asked me question and I found myself working on other people's YouTube Channels and that is when I learned what you are seeing in this book. My friends' videos started to blast off and yet I had not done the deep down work on my own YouTube Channel.

Finally Tippy decided to do a YouTube Channel. She had been helping me for years and knew most of what I knew. That is when I decided to take on my Channel and Improve it. The meta data was redone.

The problem is all the years my YouTube videos set with little meta data to help them do well. I got traffic but could have done so much better if I knew what I know now when I first started my YouTube Channel.

That is the reason Tippy and I got together to write this book. To help other YouTube Creators so they don't make the same mistake I did.

I hope it helps you.

<u>Tippy</u> :
https://www.youtube.com/channel/UCZdLD5qe6ab3YNopDahDhjA

I am a New YouTube Creator. But, I have been helping Ebonygeek45 keep up with the editing of her YouTube videos for years.

When I started my YouTube Channel earlier this year it was to help others with their YouTube Channels. That is what my YouTube Channel is about. Ebonygeek45 voices my videos.

Frankly, if not for her I would not have been as bold to start my YouTube Channel. This book is the research I put together along with things I know work from seeing YouTube Channels Ebonygeek45 worked on. I got to start my YouTube Channel with a lot of knowledge behind it. In this book we are sharing a bit of that knowledge with you.

Enjoy!!

www.ingramcontent.com/pod-product-compliance
Lightning Source LLC
Chambersburg PA
CBHW080540060326
40690CB00022B/5188